A FIRST RESPONDER'S GUIDE TO HUMAN TRAFFICKING

What You Might See and What You Should Do

By

Sylvia & Penny, A Survivor

INTRODUCTION

We have a human trafficking problem in America today.

We're talking about humans being enslaved. Thought it ended with the Emancipation Proclamation in 1863? Nope.

In America today, some 800,000 people are enslaved.

They are forced to work in situations without freedom and without pay, often in dangerous conditions.

Some are minors, some are adults.

All of them need to be freed.

Just as important, their Slavers need to be caught and prosecuted.

In your job, you meet a lot of people. You may meet an enslaved person today. **Will you recognize them?**

This workbook will teach you about human trafficking, the different kinds of trafficking, and how people fall into it. If you are a **teacher**, **EMS professional**, **transportation worker**, or **medical clinician**, be sure to read the page specific to your profession. Law enforcement personnel should familiarize themselves with all the information presented here.

 The Goal: Victim liberation and prosecution of the perpetrators.

What we can't do is show you a way to 100% guarantee you've found a trafficking victim.

Some of the signs are subtle, and some may point to other social and domestic situations. If a person presents with two or more of these symptoms, you might be looking at a victim of human trafficking, and should call the Hotline.

Awareness, education, and team work are our main weapons against trafficking, and we want you to know it all.

Human Trafficking 101

TYPES OF TRAFFICKING

Sex Labor   Labor   Babies   Porn   Organs   Domestic Servitude

Human trafficking is the use of force, fraud or coercion to exploit someone for labor or commercial sex. Any minor exploited for commercial sex is a victim of human trafficking.

You should know:

→ This form of modern-day slavery is alive and thriving all over the United States. Where rates of child poverty are high, so are the rates of victimization of children, the most vulnerable population for sex trafficking. The average age of a child sex victim is 12-14 years old. If casinos are in the area, there is high demand for commercial sex.[1]

→ Trafficking is a team effort. A loose coalition of people, motivated by old-fashioned greed, work together to keep people enslaved.

→ A pimp, whose role is similar to that of an agent, acts as a father or mother figure, often calling themselves, "Daddy," and referring to the slaves as a "family." To keep control over slaves, pimps use extreme violence on the offender or on someone the offender loves. Pimps keep their victims in a state of perpetual terror, anxiety, depression, submissiveness, and nervousness.

→ The operation is transient – wherever the money is, they go. This constant movement serves to keep victims disoriented and unable to run away. Special events, conventions, casinos, hotels, commercial brothels, residential brothels, truck stops, highways, and streets are all places where human trafficking thrives on a sharp demand. Bus/train terminals serve as recruiting grounds for runaways.

→ Traffickers take advantage of people with sex addiction, and it's a lucrative business.

The average pedophile molests 260 victims during their lifetime. [9]

HOW PEOPLE GET TRAFFICKED

Victims need something – love, basic necessities, a job, drugs, money, physical items like clothes/tech/bling, immigration, to pay a debt, to keep their family safe.

Slavers are GREEDY. They exploit the vulnerable without mercy in order to make money.

Slavers, with their team of assistants, take charge of the victim's life by kidnapping, imprisonment, physical violence, coercion (blackmail), coaxing, or selling a service (coyote, immigration lawyer). They market a victim, maintain them, discipline them, emotionally manipulate them, restrict their movement, force them to work, keep their documents and their pay.

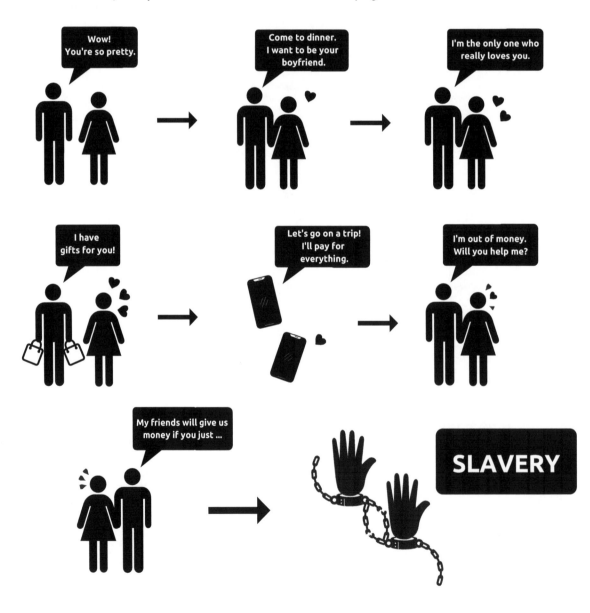

With your help, the story can end with:

Discovery

Liberation

Prosecution of Perpetrators.

WHAT HAPPENS TO PEOPLE WHEN THEY ARE TRAFFICKED

Sex trafficking is quota work. Missing a quota results in a beating. Slaves are given drugs for sex and are exhausted from constant work. Medical/dental concerns are ignored until serious. STDs, pregnancies with no pre-natal care, malnutrition, squalid living conditions, and abusive treatment are daily experiences for sex slaves. The toll on the body is so severe that most trafficked people die within seven years if they are not freed.[2]

Slaves forced to make pornography are often treated like and used as sex slaves.

Labor trafficking and domestic servitude involve long days in extreme conditions. Exhaustion from little or no sleep is often the norm. Labor and domestic slaves do not receive preventative medical or dental care, their physical needs go unmet, and, as with other slaves, abusive treatment is a daily occurrence.

Organs trafficking victims are often at the mercy of misinformation. They receive only a fraction of the money they are promised, if any, and often face a lifetime of ill health as a side-effect of their organ's removal.

Babies, some of whom are the children of slaves or victims of kidnapping, are sold to "adoption" agencies. Emotional and sometimes physical trauma are the result for the mother, as well as the baby.

SOME WAYS VICTIMS PRESENT

Not sure if what you're seeing is human trafficking? Here are some signs:

- Passive/uncommunicative – someone talks for the victim, s/he won't talk about their injury/illness, or gives a scripted or inconsistent history
- No eye-contact – when questioned, looks to Slaver or down
- No ID or money – someone else carries it for them
- Anxious – excessively concerned with pleasing Slaver
- Exhausted – they work long hours, often at night
- Suddenly altered – a recent downturn or change in clothing, grooming, speech, attitude, tech toys, ways they spend free time, grades, relationships with friends or family
- Not dressed for the weather – often in something skimpy or pajamas
- Not fully dressed – no underclothing, no shoes
- Not groomed – hair in disarray, body odor
- Missing hair, teeth
- Different gait – walking with a limp, shuffling as if in pelvic pain
- Arms around self – arms across abdomen as if guarding
- Bruising, wounds, lacerations – signs of physical abuse
- Trauma to orifices – interior or exterior damage to the body's major openings.
- Pain on urination – chronic urinary tract infection
- Tattooing – often in, on, or around genitals and breasts, neck, wrists
- Shaved – pubic hair shaved
- Not oriented – unaware of location (city they are in), date, address
- Altered Mental State – high or drunk, Slaver encourages more intoxicants
- Track marks – signs of drug use
- Unwilling to "tell on" their Slaver – brainwashed, blackmailed, emotionally manipulated, believes Slaver is good/needs them
- In constant communication with Slaver via text/phone when physically separated
- Are/were in foster care
- Experienced childhood sexual abuse
- Was/is an adolescent runaway
- Are from families with few economic resources
- Afraid of authority (EMS, LE, ED Personnel), terrified of Slaver
- Kept in by security measures in the home (outside locks, bars on windows)
- May respond in anger, be resistant to help
- Gay – almost a third of gay youth have been exploited

HOW SLAVERS AND THEIR TEAMS PRESENT

- Do all the talking, "translate," won't give victim privacy
- Claim victims cannot understand the language
- Carry victim's ID
- Claim relationship to victim
- Authoritarian/Domineering/Controlling
- Often have open shirts, with gold chains showing (seriously!)
- Try to maintain victim's intoxicated state
- Say they don't know
- Blame trouble on victim
- Have porn paraphernalia
- Have drug paraphernalia
- Confident, smooth-talkers with answers for everything
- Carry large amounts of cash
- Behave violently
- Have deep web accounts/sites
- Carry multiple cell phones
- Break minor laws
- Try to bribe
- Look normal
- Have an airtight story

QUESTIONS WHICH MAY HELP IDENTIFY VICTIMS

- Who is with you?
- Who keeps your ID/Passport?
- Have you ever run away from home?
- Have you ever traded sex for something you need? For money?
- Have you had sex with more than five partners?
- Has anyone ever forced you to have sex?
- How much sleep do you get each night?
- What is your job like? What do you get paid?
- What if you want to leave your job?
- Where are your children?

WHAT TO DO IF YOU SUSPECT HUMAN TRAFFICKING:

Call the Human Trafficking Hotline:

888.3737.888

The Hotline is free and anonymous.

If the situation turns out to be something other than human trafficking, you will not get in trouble, so call even if you're not certain.

It's important to dial the Hotline first, as human trafficking falls under federal jurisdiction.

The hotline operator will contact the FBI and its local partner agencies.

PREPARE IN ADVANCE

Help create an agency protocol that includes:

- Identification of Victims
- Treatment of Victims
- Calling the Human Trafficking Hotline
- Assisting in Liberation Efforts
- Detainment and Prosecution of Perpetrators

If your agency already has a plan in place, familiarize yourself with it.

Right now, enter the Human Trafficking Hotline number in your cell phone contacts.

Step-by-Step on the Job

EMS PERSONNEL

- Call the Human Trafficking Hotline from the scene .
- Ask law enforcement to meet you at the ED or have them ride along.
- Follow local protocols.
- Remember: a minor involved in commercial sex is a victim of human trafficking.
- Be gentle. Be compassionate. Establish rapport. Rude comments help no one.
- Use an even tone with victims – no surprise, no pity at their stories.
- Show them they are not alone.
- Explain what is happening in order to give them some control. [3]

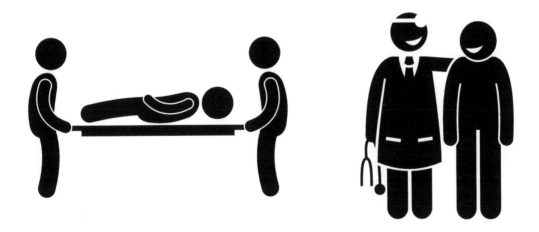

The majority of victims (88%) come in contact with a health professional during the time of their exploitation. Almost no one is recognized as a victim of human trafficking. [4]

TRANSPORTATION PERSONNEL

Ask your employer about their policy for witnessing human trafficking. Keep an eye on parking lots, truck stop stores, rest stops, bus/train stations. Look for:

- People, especially young teen girls, walking from truck to truck
- Car/truck pairing, exchanging passengers
- Physical injury/illness (see "Medical Clinicians")
- People looking for food in waste cans
- Talk of 'beavers' or 'lot lizards' among truckers
- White towel hanging from mirrors
- Flashing lights when parked
- Unusual sounds from a truck container
- Unusually large food order
- People hording condiments
- Stealing food/tech/cigs/alcohol
- A person being dropped off at truck, picked up 20 minutes later
- RVs parked in the back of the truck parking area
- A van full of young teens pulling into truck parking
- Teens arriving alone

Remember: any minor involved in commercial sex is a victim of human trafficking!

If you can have a private conversation, ask:

- Are you traveling by yourself?
- When did you last see your family?
- Are you being paid? Do you have any money?
- Are you being watched or followed?
- Are you free to move, come/go as you please?
- Are you physically or sexually abused?
- Is your family threatened? What kind of threat?

* If something feels fishy, call the hotline! It's confidential and anonymous, and you won't get in trouble if you were wrong.

* Give details – vehicle color, make, number of occupants, their race, age of girls/boys, license plate/state, driver description, and take pictures or video for evidence, if you can.

* Tell the general manager of the business on whose property the trafficking is taking place.

* Close any loopholes traffickers have taken advantage of.[5]

MEDICAL CLINICIANS

* Call the Human Trafficking Hotline.
* Ask law enforcement to meet you in the ED.
* Insist on privacy – remove the Slaver from the room.
* Use hospital translation services.
* Follow hospital protocol.
* Be gentle. Be compassionate. Establish rapport. Rude comments help no one.
* Use an even tone with victims – no surprise, no pity at their stories.
* Show them they are not alone.
* Explain what is happening in order to give them some control.
* Watch for a patient to "check out" emotionally if catheterization is necessary.
* Remember: any minor involved in commercial sex is a victim of human trafficking.
* Make a list of agencies/resources in your area – shelters, counselors, advocates – who can provide "3 hot and a cot."

Medical personnel can expect victims, especially children, to present with pediculosis, scabies, and tuberculosis. In addition, victims may present with:

- Anxiety
- Chronic pain
- Cigarette burns
- Complications from abortion
- Contusions
- Depression
- Fractures
- Gastrointestinal problems
- Headaches
- Oral health problems
- Pelvic pain
- Posttraumatic stress disorder
- Sexually transmitted infections
- Suicidal ideation
- Unhealthy weight loss
- Unwanted pregnancy
- Vaginal pain

Because the client is unlikely to identify his/herself as a trafficking victim, the provider needs to pay attention to subtle and nonverbal cues.

The provider should care for any immediate needs, including treatment of physical trauma, sexually transmitted infections, diagnosis of pregnancy, and assessing for suicidal ideation.

Next, call the Human Trafficking Hotline: 888.3737.888.

It may be helpful to pass on information about the "T Visa." The United States Department of Justice created the Trafficking Visa (T Visa) to allow the victim (and certain family members) to remain in the United States legally if the victim complies with "reasonable requests for assistance in the investigation or prosecution of acts of trafficking." Recipients of the T Visa are eligible for legal employment and can become lawful permanent residents after 3 years. [6]

Always assume this medical visit is the last. Victims are very likely to be lost to follow up due to the transient nature of their Slavers. [7]

It bears repeating:

The majority of enslaved people (88%) come in contact with a health professional during the time of their exploitation. Almost no one is recognized as a victim of human trafficking. [8]

TEACHERS

Teachers may have the opportunity to see victims during recruitment and the beginnings of exploitation. Watch for changes among the student population. Keep a protective eye out for:

- Economically-challenged kids – they are the most vulnerable
- Children who often "go home" during the day.
- Children who miss school regularly.
- A sudden change in behavior, belongings, grades, posture, eye-contact, attitude, clothing, grooming, speech, tech
- Foster children, who often have no one to protect them
- Gay students, who are at huge risk of exploitation
- Significantly older "boyfriends"
- Significant anger issues/violence
- Sexual acting out/abuse of other students
- Fear/anxiety
- Signs of physical trauma/injury
- Pornography
- Sexting

* Create a trusting environment between you and your students.

* Post the Human Trafficking Hotline number – call if you suspect something.

* Explain the grooming process to students.

* Warn about texting pictures/modeling jobs/people giving "free" gifts/parties/rape drugs.

Resources:

Truckers Against Trafficking: www.truckersagainsttrafficking.org provides training and certification for travelers/truckers who pledge to help victims and report human trafficking.

TraffickJam App (available free for iOS and Android) helps you call the Human Trafficking Hotline.

TraffickCam App (available free for iOS and Android): helps you take pictures of your hotel room to aid in prosecuting live-stream human trafficking.

Polaris Project: www.polarisproject.org information and resources about trafficking. Sponsors of the National Human Trafficking Hotline.

Thistle Farms: www.thistlefarms.org. Place of recovery for victims of human trafficking, addiction, and prostitution.

References:

1 https://inpublicsafety.com/2014/02/the-role-of-medical-responders-in-the-fight-against-human-trafficking/
2 www.mercycare.org/about/community-benefit/anti-human-trafficking/
3 https://combathumantrafficking.org/2017/12/first-responders-the-potential-to-disrupt-trafficking/
4 combathumantrafficking.org
5 truckersagainsttrafficking.org
6 https://www.ncbi.nlm.nih.gov/pmc/articles/PMC3125713/
7 https://www.amazon.com/Sex-Trafficking-Clinical-Guide-Nurses/dp/082617115X
8 combathumantrafficking.org
9 http://www.yellodyno.com/Statistics/statistics_child_molester.html

Made in the USA
Middletown, DE
13 January 2024

47614953R00015